CAROL COFFEE REPOSA
NEW AND SELECTED POEMS

Poetry Volumes by Carol Coffee Reposa

At the Border: Winter Lights (San Antonio: Pecan Grove Press, 1989)

The Green Room (San Antonio: Pecan Grove Press, 1998)

Facts of Life (Dallas: Browder Springs Press, 2002)

Underground Musicians (Beaumont: Lamar University Literary Press, 2013)

Carol Coffee Reposa
New and Selected Poems

TCU Press
Fort Worth, Texas

TCU Texas Poet Laureate Series

Library of Congress Cataloging-in-Publication Data

Names: Reposa, Carol Coffee, author.
Title: New and selected poems / Carol Coffee Reposa.
Description: Fort Worth, Texas : TCU Press, [2019] | Series: TCU Texas poet
  laureate series |
Identifiers: LCCN 2019002921 (print) | LCCN 2019004872 (ebook) | ISBN
  9780875657233 () | ISBN 9780875657226
Subjects: | LCGFT: Poetry.
Classification: LCC PS3618.E77 (ebook) | LCC PS3618.E77 A6 2019 (print) | DDC
  811/.6--dc23
LC record available at https://urldefense.proofpoint.com/v2/url?u=https-
3A__lccn.loc.gov_2019002921&d=DwIFAg&c=7Q-
FWLBTAxn3T_E3HWrzGYJrC4RvUoWDrzTlitGRH_A&r=O2eiy819IcwTGuw-
vrBGiVdmhQxMh2yxeggw9qlTUDE&m=mLiFIojuSDEEUlS42kWdbImVx9m6ICQ_WmL6Cd-
otkc&s=fa-dwkfEUh_4vtEbcM2ML7ik9e5xBC8OU284jwql_Lo&e=

TCU Press
TCU Box 298300
Fort Worth, TX 76129
817.257.7822
www.prs.tcu.edu

To order books: 1.800.826.8911

Designed by fusion29
www.fusion29.com

DEDICATED WITH immeasurable love
TO THE memory OF my mother,
Jane SHINDLer COFFee crow (1917–1999)

contents

Introduction

The world is a book and those who do not travel read only one page.
—Saint Augustine

Carol Coffee Reposa: New and Selected Poems is the twelfth volume in
the Texas Poet Laureate series published by TCU Press. These vol-
umes are a collectible sampling of the high quality of poetry that con-
tinues to be produced in Texas. The volume you now hold continues
with that tradition.

Carol Reposa is a poet you will wish you had started reading
twenty years ago. Among scores of publication credits she has ap-
peared in *The Atlanta Review* and *The Valparaiso Review*. This volume
includes poems from her volumes *At the Border: Winter Lights*, *The
Green Room*, *Facts of Life*, and *Underground Musicians*. Included also are
several new poems illustrating her continuing high quality of work.

Incomprehensible, inarticulate, and inaccessible. A false, post-
modern tone, self-indulgent, and agenda-driven. Those words and
phrases describe much of what attempts to pass for contemporary po-
etry. Poetry is in danger of losing an audience in a blind dash to be
pertinent. A lot of it is, frankly, not good. Reposa's work is the diamet-
ric opposite. Carol Reposa has long been considered to be one of the
steadfast poetic voices of Texas letters. Avoiding the labeling of poetry
schools, neither modern nor postmodern, not limited to free verse nor
rhyme and meter, not bound by the constraints of agenda, Reposa's
work exhibits clarity, accessible description, and wisdom using simple
and rich metaphor and allegory. Writing since her youth, she has
taught and edited poetry for years. While the geographic origin, or
claimed home, of a poet can influence his or her work, and sometimes
even bring along the dreaded label of "regional poet," Reposa defies
that. While she embraces and weaves her environment into her poems,
she is not limited to the geographic place where she currently resides.
She is good.

Measuring the quality of a poem can be an elusive and ephemeral
thing. Too often the quantitative is abandoned in favor of the qualita-
tive, the "I don't why it's good but I know what I like and I like this" ar-
gument. Reposa's remarkable poetry can be measured using both
quantitative and qualitative measures. Part of what makes her good is
her rich language. It is subtle and woven artfully into the fabric of her

lines. She uses incredibly rich and exact nouns, connotative adjectives, unexpected and exciting verbs. Add to that her ability to move from broad, landscape vision to minute, in-the-moment detail, and you have the hallmarks of a craftsman.

Many of her poems are written in the first person. But Reposa is smart enough to step out of the way. "One Night in a Cheap Motel" and "In Parida Cave" exhibit the same characteristic: Reposa uses the first person to set up, to define the scene—but she incorporates details and emotions we all know and understand. She makes the poems about us—not about her.

There are villanelles and sonnets and sestinas hidden in this collection, but it isn't the exhibition of skill and form knowledge that is impressive. It is the fact that she uses the forms so effortlessly.

As you read through the book it will become obvious that Reposa has more than a passing knowledge of history. Her references to events and peoples are tools to her, like her travel experiences, that she uses to illustrate our very humanity. While she may transport us into the moments of Elizabethan England (read the five-poem sonnet sequence), her looking back into history always feels immediate, as if the event just occurred, as if the memory is still strong, as if we were there. Consider these lines from "The Anne Frank House," a villanelle that is a startling and vivid description of what Anne Frank must have lived through during the Nazi occupation.

Her giant, startled eyes stretch at the strain
Of living briefly in black ink. The roar
Throws shadows on the tree that kept her sane.

Her gallery of stars, their smiles inane
And ghastly on the tattered wall, ignore
The echo of the jackboots in the rain . . .

Another example are lines from "On Charles Whitman," a poem describing the day of the sniper attack at the University of Texas in the 1960s.

He reached the observation deck,
Unpacked deodorant and rifles
Ate some lunch.
No one saw

At first
The lazy puffs of smoke, or heard
Those dull reports
That sounded like a distant fireworks show.

No one made connection
Even when the passersby
Began to melt
Along the sidewalks

Or in front of cars
And smoke kept rising
From the Tower
In languid spirals

    She uses the same techniques for her travel poems. "Lenin's
Tomb" and "Babushka's Monologue" are just two of several. This is
characteristic of a true Don Quixote—someone who has acquired
knowledge through travel—but who continues to question, think, and
write like a poet.
    As a sample, here are some lines from the poem "Love in Another
Language":

No phrase fits
The street parade in Guanajuato,
Músicos strolling down cobbles
Ten guitars smiling in a mountain night.
Nor can I translate
Fields of blue maguey
Rolling down a slope, a misplaced ocean,
Or the *malecón* in Vera Cruz
The sky a glittering hot blanket
Covering the Gulf.

    And lines from the poem "Mayan on the March":

Pacheco's mural shows the *indio's* feet,
Nothing but his feet

Their long strides raising clouds of dust
That billow through the gallery.

Calloused, seamed, without shoes
They leave their giant portrait
Walking off the canvas
Straight through me, passing through.

Passing through her. Reposa allows the images, the words to pass through her directly to the reader. A remarkable turn of phrase.

The selection of new poems in this volume exhibits another level of Reposa's continuing poetic skill. The darkly quirky and anachronistic "Lincoln in an Upscale Mall" and first-person travel poem "Venice" are especially good.

Then Reposa presents the excellent closing poem, "An Evening With Willie Nelson." She pulls in the historical metaphor of Ulysses, the epic traveler; she includes us in her own travels, in her own yearnings, when she leads us to the closing lines of

... As I too follow the sun
And sail west.

Not only has Carol Reposa had a long journey to become Texas Poet Laureate, but like Ulysses, she has also brought wisdom with her.

The Laureates represented in this series of volumes continue to prove that Texas poetry is not limited to a cattle-populated, sere, and tumbleweed-driven landscape. While those characteristics are certainly part of the Texas worldview, and, as part of the environ-ment, have made it into many a fine poem, Texas poets are not bound by fences real or literary. Carol Reposa's fine work is espe-cially indicative of this. She pays tribute to her state, but she also reaches beyond borders and comes back with words and images.

Carol Reposa is a poet you will wish you had started reading twenty years ago.

Sit down and start turning pages. It's time to catch up.

Alan Birkelbach
Editor, TCU Texas Poet Laureate Series

I

Poems from *At the Border: Winter Lights*

THE Anne Frank House

The echo of the jackboots in the rain,
The studded leather splintering the door
Throws shadows on the tree that kept her sane.

Her fragile profile, two thin hands remain,
The shadow of her shoulders hunched before
The echo of the jackboots in the rain.

Her giant, startled eyes stretch at the strain
Of living briefly in black ink. The roar
Throws shadows on the tree that kept her sane.

Her gallery of stars, their smiles inane
And ghastly on the tattered wall, ignore
The echo of the jackboots in the rain

Until they hear the jagged, sharp refrain
Of sirens. Then the pounding on the floor
Throws shadows on the tree that kept her sane.

The flimsy bookcase hacked, the end made plain,
Deciphered in the barbed wire past the store:
The echo of the jackboots in the rain
Throws shadows on the tree that kept her sane.

HILL COUNTRY REST HOME

At the fort the flag flies all night long.
Inside the cold stone rooms
Are broken lanterns,
Gusts of wind, Comanche arrows
Memories of spurs and flint,
Dingy photographs of Johnston, Thomas, Lee
Behind cracked glass.

From this rise a visitor sees everything:
The tired kaleidoscope
Of storefronts faced in river rock
Tile rooftops, stunted trees
And lines of slowly moving cars.

Beyond the hills
I hear the muffled roar of cannon,
Underbrush snapped
By rag-wrapped, bleeding feet
In quick retreat,
A tattered blanket thrown across the back,
Dead dreams ripping at the brain.

Below are rusty pickups,
Tidy hospitals
Retirement homes to house the ghosts
Of other wars
While somewhere
Just before the morning medication
After all the doors are locked,
The General surrenders
To the yuccas and bluebonnets,
While scores of wrinkled soldiers
Hobble on to Appomattox.

For my mother

You look fragile now,
A sigh in shapeless white
That tosses, rail to rail, in your iron bed,
Your door just like the other doors
That open on a road of disinfected tile
While monitors continue flickering,
Lost messages
Inscrutable
On rows of gray-black screens.

But I remember
When you clubbed a diamondback to death,
Sun glinting off the hissing writhing skin
At even angles
Like the motion of your arms
Across the lake,
Your body locked in measured reaching
As it pulled blue distance into breath,
A song in icy water.

And I remember
When you pounded Gershwin
On our dreary spinet,
Filling rooms with city lights
And scores of red silk gowns.

The old piano now lies mute.
I touch it briefly
But my hands sigh helplessly
From key to key
And I must stop
To listen
For the rustle of red silk.

MY UNCLE'S SONG

"Take me out to the ball game . . . "

I look down at the body, muscles stiff,
The eyelids faintly swollen. Cheeks and chin
Are rouged—a tired old Rubens, sated, lips
Set in the smallest smile. Hands touch the pin
Striped vest, arrange once more the stubby fingers
Into proper folds. He's ready then.

"Take me out to the crowd . . . "

Red rose in his lapel, the red wine lingers
In his glass, his smile reflected in
Its curves. The song is his. So many singers,
Though. The steward brings the *coq au vin*,
Presents it French-style on his arm, a white
Starched cloth beneath. We drink and sing till dawn.

"Buy me some peanuts and Crackerjacks . . . "

The maître d' brings me a hurricane light,
Extinguishes the flame and puts a rose
Inside the glass. It burns beyond the night
Until, the street lamps shrinking into bows
Unstrung and limp, we fall into the car,
The slick white Cadillac. Our singing grows.

"I don't care if I never get back . . . "

Red wine racing past the stars,
White-top Cadillac careening lane
To lane, from left to right, no skid or jar
Permitted in the waltz-time swerves, the rain
Fall silent at the start, my uncle smooths
His red silk tie and drives us home again.

"So it's root, root, root for the home team . . . "

His voice rising clear above the hues
Of early morning, lavishly he sings
Extravagant old tunes that bind their truths
In tight end-rhymes and closest harmonies,
In praise of cloudless skies and rose-banked walls,
Where brave and guileless men think noble things.

"If they don't win it's a shame . . . "

In some oblique career among the shells,
On some cold field a few miles past Bastogne
My uncle gathers shattered limbs, impels
A shredded arm into position, bone
Placed neatly in its socket, stitched so close,
But drinks his heavy burgundy alone.

"So it's one, two, three strikes you're out . . . "

His last day is redundant. Doomed by those
Hard gifts and his relentless giving, he
Is not surprised. We pin a dark red rose
In his lapel, arrange so carefully
The red silk tie. The priest sifts thick red clay
On top. We lower him into memory.

"At the old ball game . . . "

The Spanish moss dips down in languid play
Above the soft red earth as dull clouds shear
Off light between the leaves, the old oaks gray
In falling light. And one last time we hear
The echo of those gallant sunset songs
That finished him, while slowly night appears.

serenade

for my grandparents

I never heard them talk of anything
Except the scarcity of decent help,
Low prices for their cotton, times to pick
Wild plums, perhaps the latest outrage in
The city. Never did they talk about
Transcendence, squabble over Emerson
Or even Shakespeare. I was young, and so
I never listened for their quiet songs,
Their whispers drifting through the transom with
Low lamplight and a scent of talc, until
I stumbled once into their dreams, groped at
Their bedroom door with some now lost request.
I saw them lying face to face, their spent
Shapes tangled in the sheets. She was smiling,
Almost shy, her hair fanned out around
Her face, one speckled hand closed tight in his,
The scar from her new surgery still bright
Along her neck. His eyes were closed, his head
Thrown back, the grizzled curls still damp, his life
Beyond the reach of grinding steel, of sun
And rumbling cotton trucks, the only sound
The humming of the ceiling fan above
Their heads. I closed the door but still could hear
The lazy ballad of slow-moving blades
Revolving, singing, in the summer night.

II

Poems from *The Green Room*

CICADAS

They come here every August,
Butternut armies
Camping in the sycamores
Breaking up the stillness
With their drum rolls
Throbbing in the dust
And dead-end heat,
Their brief maneuvers
Carried out in clattering waves
And overlapping tides,
A corps of offbeat castanets
Not quite in sync
Until September
When their cadences
Grow fainter,
Slow almost
To a crawl.

Later we will find
Abandoned instruments,
Their ragged traps
On flowers, fences, leaves.
We search for sound.

COTTON GIN

for Cecil and Douglas

The long months used to bleach us like the cotton
In the fields. They shriveled mornings on
Their stalks and left us with the blinding white
Of sun and puffy clouds. My grandfather
Would run the vast machines from early light
To deepest night. He pulled the boiling snow
From metal teeth and filled the air with oil
That glowed along the dirt, above the trees.
Grandmother kept the books and ledgers while
I watched. Then cotton trucks would lumber off
Toward night, unpainted shacks and heavy meals,
But still the work went on. His helpers dwarfed
Him, two black giants whose muscles rippled down
Their arms and backs in chocolate waves, rose from
Their chests in glowing hills. They seldom spoke.
They heard Grandfather's words before they turned
To sound and knew all magic, even dark
Oaths muttered by the big steel teeth, the deep
And secret charges running underneath.
They levitated iron-bound bales, five hundred
Pounds of fragrant white, abundant as
The Queen Anne's lace that sprawled around the lot
And prayed all day outside the roaring walls.
One day Grandfather hit ungrounded wire.
The secret currents shot him off the floor
Floating him toward places out of reach.
The teeth kept at their tugging. But before
Grandfather drifted out of time, in motion
Quick as light one giant found and pulled
The switch, a mountain moving faster than a thought.
My grandfather dreamed on the silent floor.
They bore him, weightless as a flower, to his
Own bed. My grandmother brought doctors for
Her husband, salts and tea, gave presents to
The prophets, shining hills that knew the news

Before it came, steep slopes that sheltered fields
From frost and searing wind, that lifted seeds
Into the brightest prayers of Queen Anne's lace.

III

Poems from *Facts of Life*

paperweight

Their faces shimmer through the yellowed glass
My mother polished free of twelve years' dust,
Red powder coating everything inside
His shop, the fine grit crushed and ground from slabs
Of Brazos walnut. No one ever knew
Just why her father garnered these old icons—
Whittier, Emerson, Riley, and Longfellow—
In a makeshift shrine of shavings, small
Dreams scattered on his work table, enclosed
By dark red beams, the warm screech of his saws.
That color filtered everything: the clamps
And T-squares, planes, plumbs and lathes.
He must have needed those old poets to show
Him other colors, shade the strong designs
That curled from his gnarled fingers, anchoring
The epithets that streamed like sweat through all
Those years, that poured into the fine four-posters,
Desks and beveled sideboards in that space.

Today his prophets gather light and time
On my oak desk. Their old lines burn. I lift
The glass and half expect to see it blur
Into a nautilus, each chamber round
And roaring with its distant sounds, a song
That pours, dark red, into my waiting hand.

OLD CLOCK

My mother lived by its soft strokes, began
Her life while its long pendulum made time,
The brass disc sweeping side to side and year
To year while she endured her long piano
Lessons, met young men, crawled up the squeaky
Stairs when she had missed her curfew. It
Was chiming when her brother drew his first
Breath, and his last. The large hands moved when all
The stores were closed for the Centennial
And cotton gins dissolved into bare lots
Where melons burst on every vine. Its heart
Beat steadily through every grudging turn
Of its brass key and several coats of paint
Through all the silent winters, noisy springs.

Today it is arrhythmic, fibrillating
Daily, striking twice at noon, ten times
At one. But still my daughter hears it when
She comes in late. My son consults it hours
Before each game. I've peeled away the paint
To find New England pine that might have filled
A stand somewhere in Massachusetts, tall
And fragrant, branches growing steadily
Through all the silent winters, noisy springs.

naturaL woman

for Ruth

Long after all the honky-tonks had closed,
Beery tenors headed for the street
Lamps in every tidy neighborhood put out,
My baby always woke,
Frightened at the lack of light,
Shrieks arching through the hours
Like lasers.

Then we'd walk the floor,
My footfall tracing circuits on the rug
Her damp head stiff
Fists clenched
Until I raised the volume on the radio
And she could hear
The late-night songs
That warmed the dark,
Enfolding her like blankets.

We would dance across the living room
Into the kitchen
Back again,
Aretha Franklin telling her
In tones that shimmered like cut glass
That she was natural
Night was fine,
And dark made possible
The shining of the stars.

At last my daughter slept,
Her head collapsed
Arms draped loosely round the songs
That brought light to the room
And then I could return her to the night,
A waiting bed
The soft, enfolding dark.

Great Horned Owl

for Cash

He swooped into our yard at dusk
Heavy with the smell of coming rain,
Settling on the topmost branch
Of a decaying tree
Still studded with pecans.
The dogs went wild
Pawed at the trunk
Howled like Furies.

I watched for magic light,
Reflections of lost places
Glowing in his eyes
But he did nothing, stayed above us
Calm as a marble bust
While darkness gathered in his wings,
A silhouette in charcoal
One shade deeper than the night.

Almost fused with evening,
He started to unfurl
In secret, languid ritual
The way someone might raise a flag
When no one else could see,
Stiff fabric flapping several times
In lumbering majesty
Before he lofted slowly into stars.

In Parida Cave

I view the paintings
Through a chain link fence, a wall
Of perfect interlocking diamonds,
Barbed wire looped across the top
In stiff festoons. Beyond
Are other walls and diamonds,
Geometric prayers brushed over limestone
Centuries ago,
Growing slowly
Through the storms
And blue-white afternoons
Along the Pecos.

Dwellers must have rested here
Before and after every hunt,
Watching through the night
Around flames high enough
To blacken even these damp walls
Heavy with their clumps of maidenhair
And wild tobacco, strawberry cactus
Sprouting just above. They might have seen
The spirals swept by hundreds of blue herons
Circling the rookery, giant turtles
Swimming through their centuries
Of stone. They would have heard
The wind rise when the northers came.

Today the cave is mute,
A darkened palimpsest
Of points and fire rocks,
Bones and ancient blood,
Its topmost layer
Covered with new leavings:
Beer cans, bottle tops, and cigarettes
Settling slowly in the midden
With the other relics, paint gangs
From abandoned railroads leaving names

In block print three feet high,
Later tags from the Blades and Crips.

Further down the river
Lightning strikes a shaman's arm,
Burning it into the rock.
His hand bursts
Above the water line,
Contours stretched with light.
My fingers tighten on the wire.

TECHNICAL DIFFICULTIES

for Don

We experience them
From birth,

Those small Fifth Columnists
Wriggling through our lives,
Setting down the pegs
That make our music:
Forceps not quite fitting
Fragile heads,
Nipples clogged with sour milk
Tricycles that rust
In carports
Banal banana peels
Left waiting on the sidewalk.

Later on,
The thousand natural shocks
Make static on the radio,
Stall cars along the Interstate
At 5:00,
Those endless bottlenecks
Brownouts, blackouts,
Sleek transformers
Bursting in the heat,
Arias that end
A half-step flat.

Lords of Misrule,
They will inch into our finest hours.
Hijacked honeymooners, rendezvous
Forever gone awry,
Fathers who can't make it
To the hospital
Before the baby comes,

Best men who forget
The ring,
Messages that don't reach Romeo
In time.

Misdirected Bacchae,
They will dog our deaths:
Lodging chicken bones in windpipes,
Tearing air from lungs
Pulling life from hearts
Thickening the blood
Or thinning it
Until the vessels swell
And finally pop
At breakfast time
Or during someone's bath

While we
Stand by.

A Sestina on Greed

It oozes from the TV screens like oil,
Gushes up into the living room
Leaves slick on rugs and furniture,
Drapes the greenbacks of material girls
In velvet, mink, whatever they might want
To wear inside the malls.

A wheel of fortune spins in board rooms, malls,
Hurls seals, whales, gulls, and oil
Along the beach, while CEOs want
Ladies gliding by in noble furs, brass madonnas in a room
That looks out on the skyline, call girls
Waiting for the ring that adds them to the furniture.

And in Brazil, forests fall for furniture
Enhancing corporate suites or glowing in the malls
Where Krugerrands and diamonds are forever. Pearl girls
Sign on every line, buy oil
To keep their faces smooth. The shops make room
For everything they want

And need: ivory necklaces to shelter them from want,
Alligator handbags crafted from the useless furniture
Of swamps, stilettos in the Everglades which still have room
For harvesting, wetland malls
Sadly overstocked with so much oil
A few miles out. Botox girls

Flash blinding smiles for more, as girls
Of every color have more fun with Testarossas. Men want
Trumps, a Swiss account with laundered sheets, oil
Of enterprise along the border, furniture
Of buy-outs, sell-outs in those backstreet malls
Where you can find the old familiar splits, and room

For traffic, time and room
To cut the finest deal, heads and players, babes and girls

In toylands stocked with every kind of rig, while malls
Crank out machines to sell the soda, cola, coke, want
Of many telescoped to red DeLoreans and other furniture
Designed for ecstasy and oil.

The business of America is making room and want
Available to all the boys and girls, all their furniture
For sale in malls that float in blood and oil.

APOSTROPHE TO THE CAPTORS

for Amnesty International

That man who languishes in concrete—
He's my brother.

And the one with fruit flies in his mouth—
He drank with me,
While someone played the violin.

That child whose fingers bend in all directions—
She's my own.
I labored hours with her
One summer afternoon.

And that woman with the marks of pipes
Along her face—
She fed me sandwiches each afternoon.
She walked the floor with me
When I fell ill.
She also walked with you.
She talked to you
When no one else would speak.
She took you in her arms
When you had drunk too much.

And if you hit her
One more time,
Don't be surprised
If fruit flies trickle from your lips,
If current burns your flesh
To cinders that a vulture wouldn't touch
And if
When you have thudded into sleep
As heavy as lead pipes
You see yourself with welts across your face,
Eyes popping from your brow

For all those lives that suffer—
They are yours.

For Anne Bradstreet

She must have felt the hard wind cut between
The planks and rattle makeshift desks while she
Conceived her rambling children, ink-stained, seen
And heard, their chirping loud in every tree
That rooted in her yard, the branches bare
Except for all that twittering. The stare

Of Elders sometimes must have slowed her, stopped
The scandal for a while. Perhaps she marched
To meeting stiff in white lace collars, dropped
Her gaze demurely during prayers starched
And solemn for the Sabbath while she planned
The next small outrage brooding in her hand.

She must have plotted while she cut wood, set
The corn and milked the cows, put up preserves,
The faces of her imps enough to whet
The carping tongues that needled her, sharp curves
On which her feet might slide. But still she bore
Those small plump shapes, each one the molten core

Of yet another mating. Even when
Her house burned she was thinking of the next
Long night, her fingers set to draw the thin
White curtains round her bed, her spirit flexed
To brave more labors, showing in the streets,
To meet her Saint between the freezing sheets.

Grading in Las Vegas

for Richard

Sitting in our red hotel room
I shut out the crimson carpet,
Miles of neon, quarters jingling
By the millions in casinos
While I mark the essays for that week,

Plodding through a score of fragments
In their ragged choruses
Vaudeville introductions
Dog-and-pony paragraphs,
The tired reprise
Of twenty-five identical conclusions.

But this city won't accept my work:
A sequined thigh rips through the wall,
Gold stiletto
Puncturing
A red balloon someone had painted
Just above the bed. At first
I can ignore her,
Counting comma splices
While she belts out numbers, pink plumes
Bobbing in the air,
Her smile a vast digression
Earrings dangling to her shoulders,
Modifying everything.

I am hunting
For a dozen missing antecedents,
Defusing clauses
When she starts to dance,
Red pasties jiggling in the margins
Breasts in perfect parallel.
I can't resist her grammar
So I leave my papers,

Follow her into the streets
Notice that my dress is far too short,
Too tight
For anything
Except the dance floor
Or a swaying walk along the Strip.

FACTS OF LIFE

The fiber optics make it all look cosmic:
Sperm like warheads, eggs like planets
Whirling in their milky galaxies
Waiting for the aliens to come.

Yet this attack is poignant:
Three hundred million swimmers
Shot into an acid sea,
Their numbers shrunk to hundreds, then to scores.

A few will beat the heat, strung out
Like cyclists wriggling up a cliff
On some exhausting tour,
The pack left miles behind

Or marathoners panting up a hill
Hitting walls
Collapsing on the roadside,
Cutting loss.

A few reach journey's end.
One weary missile hits the target,
Plunges home.
And now the occupation starts

A new regime that changes everything,
Demanding constant growth
The quotas greater every day
Until at last a reddened cry
Begins another war.

IV

Poems from *Underground Musicians*

COLORS OF THE MEXICAN COAST

Hunger is the shade
Of lemon sherbet
Or a slice of watermelon.

People speak in tones
Of mango or papaya,
Dispute a price

In iridescent red like parrots' plumes,
Their voices hard
As scales on an iguana.

Sweat ripens in the lanky palms
Like coconuts,
Glazes streets in pale green drops

Or burns
In orange flames
Like blossoms on a *jacaranda*.

A child grows up
In broken cinderblocks
Blue as the rivers

He has never seen
One mile from a banana palace,
Glass-topped walls as bright

As white paint
On the trunks of trees.
Later, in a turquoise dusk

Tiles fall from roofs
In streams of cinnabar.
Then night swirls in, black

And pierced with stars
Before the colors
Start again.

MAYAN ON THE MARCH

Pacheco's mural shows the *indio's* feet,
Nothing but his feet
Their long strides raising clouds of dust
That billow through the gallery.

Calloused, seamed, without shoes
They leave their giant portrait
Walking off the canvas
Straight through me, passing through

Four centuries of hunger in the heat,
Weight no one could carry
Thirst never satisfied
Sweat rolling into an early grave

But the *indio* outlasts his journey
Continues his long march
Through deserts, saw-toothed mountains
Boiling coasts

Toward a street
Filled with song,
Marimbas playing in the dappled light,
At last cold water in the shade.

LOVE IN ANOTHER LANGUAGE

for Nicho

I have no words
For the smile
Of a ten-year-old
Who brings me coffee and a *quesadilla*
Or the sobs in a *balada*
Weeping from the radio
Or the guide
Who throws me
From the path of a Corvette
Careening down a narrow street.

No phrase fits
The street parade in Guanajuato,
Músicos strolling down cobbles
Ten guitars smiling in a mountain night.
Nor can I translate
Fields of blue maguey
Rolling down a slope, a misplaced ocean,
Or the *malecón* in Vera Cruz
The sky a glittering hot blanket
Covering the Gulf.

My dictionary offers nothing
For the Sierras all around us
Hovering like watchful mothers,
Or the random songs of windchimes
In a storm. No verb conveys the motion
Of our bus floating through the clouds
In the Tuxtlas. No noun contains
The limestone castles of Palenque,
Emerald sweat in the jungle, *escaleras*
On a pyramid, a Mayan's silent stride.

And when I collapse on a Saltillo street
I can't articulate

The man who drags me to a taxi,
Then the hospital,
Or the flower-like nurse
Who strokes my face,
Preps my arm, finds the vein
Just in time
And sits with me while I dream
Of everything that I can't say.

coca chewer in a quito museum

He's still addicted
After fifteen centuries,
That beatific gaze
Caught in time
And non-glare glass.

He cradles a small bowl
Once filled with something
Gods would want
Absolute contentment in his eyes,
That tell-tale lump in the jaw

Like a big-league pitcher
Focused on a perfect point
Beyond the catcher
Just before he throws another strike.

I think of vanished hands,
Careful fingers shaping
Rounding out the terra cotta limbs
To please a pantheon
That gathered somewhere

In the sky or sun or moon.
Track lights catch
The bearer's tranquil face, unblemished
After dusty epochs he spent buried
In the *altiplano*.

As we leave
I almost feel
That old ceramic bowl
In my embrace,
A tell-tale swelling in my jaw.

Galapágos Soap Opera

for Ethan

The cormorants
Are young and restless
Chasing everything on fat webbed feet
Water dripping from their flightless beaks.
Further out
Sea turtles gambol in the waves

Make love a hundred hours at a time.
While they are losing sleep
Father hawks must raise their young alone
Because their faithless mates have flown
To build their blended homes
In foreign *palo santo* trees.

Penguins marry and remarry
At unearthly rates,
Waddle through their noisy court dates
As the waves roll in
And the world turns.
Voyeurs in some episodes

Iguanas smolder in their scales.
They have everything it takes
For a ménage à trois,
But on a less progressive beach
Sea lions bark and screech
Eight days a week

If even one contender
Flops up on a rock
To plot
His next move on the harem.
In another torrid cove, the sally-lightfoot crabs
Are round-heeled in their quest

To keep up with the albatrosses
Who show off in daily rituals
Of afternoon delight and clattering lust,

Tête-à-tête and beak to beak

While gaggles of blue-footed boobies watch
And sibling rivalry goes unchecked

Around the dinner table
Dotted with abandoned eggs
And empty nests.
Night falls
But just like sands in the hourglass,
The sagas

Of these wings and whiskers
Scales and feathers
Glassy eyes and guano
Will continue
On these sunbaked islands
All the days of their lives.

LOS AMANTES DE SUMPA

First she died
And then he died
Ten thousand years ago.

She was twenty.
He was twenty-five.
Both were well off for their time.

Mourners laid him next to her,
Placed his arm around her waist,
His leg across her thigh.

This man and woman
Could have watched the sun
Come up each day

In bursts of red and gold
Or listened for the early morning birdsong
While they thatched their roof.

Perhaps they married,
Had a feast.
She might have borne a child.

I look at all the tangled bones
His skull crushed
Under centuries of earth

Hollows of their eyes
Filled long ago with bright desire,
What remains of him still turned to her.

It doesn't matter
When they died
Or why, or how.

All that counts this afternoon
Or any other
Is his arm around her waist,
His leg across her thigh.

ELIZABETH I on Her Parents

The King does not admit my birthright, turns
Away when Kat calls his attention to
My clothes, just as he never heard the blue
Seas ringing in my mother's laugh. He learns
All tongues with ease and grace, reads Greek, discerns
The dark red vintages, but never knew
The iron force of her queenly vows, nor drew
A sigh when suppliant, she trampled ferns
At Greenwich, wept before the court, to plead
A frugal mercy. I was in her arms,
My hair a flame against her breast. But soon
They took her to those darkened rooms. No moon
Shed light along those turrets. No alarms
Were struck. The stones consumed her. Still I bleed.

ELIZABETH I on THE DEATH OF EDWARD VI

My sweet consumptive king reigns from his bed,
His face as white and secret as a pearl,
The surface growing slowly in a curl
Of sand enclosed in a lost sea. Hopes fed
On stars and trumpets at his birth are shed
In ink and secret signings or a furl
Of crackling parchment while my prayers still swirl
Before his eyes, lost letters at his head,
Words spent. I know he will recall the fine
Red brick of Hatfield, chrisms carried, long
Bright books, green leaves we read. While God's grace still
Endows his breath, he'll know. Despite the chill
Hands of Northumberland, the hungry throng
Of crowns and thrones, his last words will be mine.

ELIZABETH I Leaving The Tower For Her Coronation

My legs grow stiff with this much kneeling, prayers
That cut through purple velvet like the claws
Of ancient lions opening their jaws
To Daniel, turning, pacing in their lairs
In blank desire to have the blood and cares
Of all that does not crouch within the laws
Of amber flanks and manes, the leap that mauls
Before it tears a slender throat. The stares
Of these black stones reach past my days to cries
And whispers, pleas and fragile arms, sounds bent
Into the corners of this cell. But I
Will carry them into the streets. The sky
Will blaze with voices, jewels that weep, the glint
Of cheers and blessings caught in ermine eyes.

ELIZABETH I On The Defeat Of The Armada

Spain's raised her swords, but I'll outlast them all.
"I have the heart and stomach of a king,"
I vowed. My fighters cheered, the ring
Of massed deep voices echoing the fall
Of Parma from his armored cliff, the call
Of iron to wood and flesh. It rose to fling
A pebble rippling to Rome, to sling
New tides along French beachfronts, made Spain small.
For them I honor stars, each ragged flame,
Even the fireships staggering across
The Channel in the night like drunks along
Rough cobbles, though I sickened at the strong
Dark smell of blood and drowning horses, loss
Of thought, of all. But still I honor flame.

ELIZABETH I ON HER APPROACHING DEATH

Outside the branches creak beneath the weight
Of winter and lost leaves, but even this
Sound, all, will soon subside into a hiss
Caught up in time and swept beyond the gate
Of what I know. I cannot keep the state
In plenty now. I've sold my jewels. The kiss
Of velvet robes is brutal and remiss.
It cuts my back. I stumble, read my fate
In the gold ring my servants had to break
Because it grew into my hand. The men
At Richmond beg for me to talk. I thirst
And do not speak. My best words burst
Out forty years ago. They made my judges thin:
"Have a care for my people." My hands shake. . . .

LENIN'S TOMB

We surrender
Everything
Before we can approach

The monolith in red and black,
Porphyry and granite
Rising from the cobbles

In a permanent epiphany
While armed guards
Order silence, lead us

Down those darkened stairs
That flow like arteries
Straight from their heart

A glass sarcophagus
Encasing one small shape
Of history, one artifact,

Its edges sealed from everything
Waxy features fixed
Beneath their crystal coffin

Change arrested
Underneath the carefully directed
Light, bright center

In a labyrinth
Of dark, the tight face
Absolute, small cheekbones

Slanting toward the past
And future, East and West
Enfolding difference

Like the double-headed eagle
Of the Romanovs,
Their old imperial seal

More like them
Than he could have guessed
While people tiptoe by the shrine

And later speak
Of burying old icons
From his century

Which rests
Immobile
Underneath the probing light.

BABUSHKA'S MONOLOGUE

I don't like the Metro, dark caves filled
With hurrying and noise, those moving stairs
That make me dizzy, but the steel cars
Rock me back and forth the way the wind
Once pushed me through tall grass outside Zagorsk
Where I grew up, the woods alive with bees
And small white butterflies, white birches high
As Nizhni's Kremlin, flowers everywhere.
I learned to use a scythe and work a plow
On days that stretched like crosses on the tops
Of domes. My father said that loving earth
Was all. But here it's dust all summer, grit
That settles in the creases of my face
And fingers, even lines my sleeves. I dream
Of cold that cleanses street and sky, sweeps all
Heat's leavings with its stiff white broom and soothes
The eyes. When snow comes, I make soup for young
Natasha, sheathe her in red scarves and coats
Each morning, bless her as she leaves for school.
She sleeps with me. I listen to her sounds,
Her quiet breathing, pull the blankets tight
To keep her warm. The older girl attends
Four classes at the University,
Wears perfume and short skirts, spends hours before
Our new machine that sews where she makes up
Sheer blouses like the ones you see in fine
Stores for the rich. Her hair shines in the sun.
She says my face is lined and rubs thick cream
Along my neck to make the wrinkles fade.
I laugh and keep my kerchief on. In our
Old days of Terror no one went to church
But now I go two times a week. I hear
The chants and smell the incense, pray to all
The saints who listen in their holy rooms
Although the noise here may drown out my words.

Maybe they do not know what happens hour
By hour in daylight, by the kiosks, streets
And stairs, so now I cross myself each time
I pass the holy gates, touch sainted walls
And think about these things while I am on
The train, its motion rocking me the way
I did my children once. Sometimes I still
Feel tall grass swirling, dancing at my knees.

FIre-GILDING ST. Isaac's

This dome,
Third largest in Eurasia
Dazzles trees, sky, even the sun.

Our guide explains "galvanoplasty."
Application of an alloy formed of gold
And mercury, shimmering liquid
Brushed on solid surfaces
Then set to flame.
The mercury burns off,
Gold now bonded to its base.

We also learn
About the sixty quitrent serfs,
Bonded slaves
Who burned off too,
Their fevers rising in a sheen
To make this dome
Blaze in the mist

Its poison necessary
And inevitable
To create a perfect circle,
Ring of God
More gold
Than Jordan, Troy
Even the Promised Land.

Tourists look straight up,
Their whispers rising
In a vapor toward the top.

STREET SYMPHONY, ST. PETERSBURG

Melodies begin
At midnight
When the crew arrives
To haul away the trolley
And repair the track
Outside my window,
Curses and jackhammers
Rising through the dark
In a furious duet.

Morning brings
A shrill aubade
Of diesels whining over bridges
In their acrid caravans.
Trams clatter through our breakfast
Ragged fanfares erupt
In our kasha
And arpeggios of squeaking doors
Drop in our tea.

Later, we bang pavement
Watch guards start a fugue
With housemaids
Followed by a screaming voluntary
While babushkas groan
At the price of everything
And a motley band
Blares "Dixie" for the Alabama tourists
As their sleek bus rolls away.

Finally, at twilight
When we want to blow up everything
Some nun or monk, invisible
Inside the battered walls,
Begins to ring the bells for vespers
And we stop
Arrested
Fuses in our hands
To hear the changes,
Old hymns
Glowing in the night.

THE VIRGIN OF VLADIMIR

Our guide
Describes the icons in detail:
Application of gold leaf on linden,
Pigments blended
Into red
And otherworldly blue,
Shapes stretched to holiness.

Suddenly I feel
The presence
Of a woman's gaze.
I find her
Set in glass, gold-flecked,
A single panel
In a single room.

Her eyes command me,
Keep me watching
While she thinks about her baby,
Lost completely
In his bright new life,
No interest in the visitors
Who shuffle through her world.

She knows,
Accepts already
Just how brief his time will be.
Already he's a man,
His head almost as large
His arms as long
As those that cradle him.

He too sees
How little time there is
To touch, to look,
To think of anything
Except his pitiless ascent,
Knowledge flat and unambiguous
As her red robe.

He reaches toward his mother,
Puts one arm around her neck.
His perfect fingers stroke her face
As for a while
He seeks
And finds
Protection from Gethsemane.

April in Pharr

for Patty and Helmut

Wind lifts the land:
Sunflowers take off
In all directions,
Bougainvillea ascending from trashcans
Palm fronds rattling above dusty streets.
The neighbor's moonbounce
Tugs at its moorings.
Even the noontime siren
Floats up in an endless spiral.

Everything starts to fly:
Raptures of chachalacas
Aubades of whippoorwills
Parliaments of jays and green parrots
Golden-throated woodpeckers and kiskadees
Chirping on telephone wires
In grapefruit and olive trees
As they start the pilgrimage.

In the end,
We all grow wings,
Sprout bedraggled feathers
Just enough to lumber east
Toward the Gulf,
Flapping awkwardly
Above the fields of levitating cabbages
Heading slowly toward a weighty world
Of clumsy pelicans
And punk-rock gulls.

A NIGHT on padre island

Flat on my back, sand wedged
Between my teeth, fogging my ears
Sandcrabs burrowing around my toes
I thought I would grow into the beach,
Root a stand of ghost-gray sunflowers.
I would become a dune, Lot's wife
In another place.

Instead I gazed
Straight up
Into a storm of light.
The sky rained stars that night
Constellations pouring on my head.
The Little Dipper ladled blue and yellow
Through the dark,
Drenched my gritty quilt.

I woke next morning
To a perfect calm
The sun well up
But still felt stars,
Their burning edges
Everywhere.

Vegetable Love in Texas

for Dick

Gardeners say
There are two things
Money can't buy:
Love and homegrown tomatoes.

I pick them carefully.
They glow in my hands, shimmer
Beneath their patina of warm dust
Like talismans.

Perhaps they are.
Summer here is a crucible
That melts us down
Each day,

The sky a sheet of metal
Baking cars, houses, streets.
Out in the country
Water-starved maize

Shrivels into artifacts,
A desiccated cache
Of shredded life.
Farmers study archeology

In limp straw hats.
But still I have
This feeble harvest,
Serendipity in red

Red like a favorite dress
Warm like a dance
Lush like a kiss long desired,
Firm like a vow, the hope of rain.

LINES COMPOSED IN THE COMPUTER CLASSROOM

We're studying discs tonight.
Like Adam made anew
I wander through this cyber garden
Paradise of facts
Naming files, opening and closing them,
Eating their strange fruit.

But soon I fall.
Seduced by thoughts of sleep
I drift
And suddenly
I'm in a wilderness of icons
Where the files can't go.

I stumble on the Internet
And open "Tennyson."
At first I am regaled
By subtle arguments
On the Laureate's long life,
His friendships, labored love.

Then by accident
(Or is it serpents in the monitor?)
The loss of Hallam seems too much.
I hit something
And a hundred Dow-Jones quotes
Explode onto the screen.

It's too late
For fortunes to be made and lost.
I seize the mouse
And click "escape,"
Thinking of the garden just outside,
Redolent of pine, thick with silent stars.

ONE NIGHT IN A CHEAP MOTEL

Here, J. Alfred Prufrock
Might have started over,
Where flocks of pudgy pigeons
Waddle toward the dumpster
In a steady progress
As evening spreads its streams
Of red and gold
Across a half-deserted parking lot.

Inside, my feet stick
To gummy carpet. Freight trains pass
Through the room each hour,
The fury of their whistles
Shaking the faded print of Sorrento
Above my bed, and missile beer cans
Hurtle through open windows,
Disturb the universe.

No one here is etherized.
A tomcat sits by my door, courting me
In plaintive yowls. Doors lock and unlock
All night long, and through the walls
I hear disembodied laughter, sultry tones
Set to raucous country-western songs.
In the room above, people come and go,
Probably not talking of Michelangelo.

The sun rises
On legions of bottles
Upright on the window sills
Or sprouting in the grass
Like amber weeds, while roughnecks
And their eager families,
Already smelling of the sea,
Load buckets, toys and towels
In their pickups for a day at the beach.
I almost hear the mermaids sing.

SONG FOR NEW ORLEANS

to the victims of Hurricane Katrina

Walt Whitman would love you
Even more today,
Grimy jewel of the South
Glowing in the foil
Of Big Muddy.
He would walk all over you,
Count the red brick buildings
Rich with soot,
Streets bright with the heavy confetti
Of shopping bags and flyers.

He would amble
Through the French Quarter,
Paint peeling from its facades
Its telephone wires sheathed in vines
Before he wolfed down gumbo in big bowls,
Crab claws floating on top like mermaids
Ever-present as flashing breasts.
He would swallow Louie Armstrong's highest notes,
Gulp down jazz and zydeco
Breathe in the ghosts of Williams and Capote

Before he strolled Canal Street
Standing on the neutral ground
To take in multitudes:
The young man rapping on a corner
A harried intern racing to the hospital,
Handcuffed teens
Piling out of the police van
Like reluctant clowns.
Maybe he would see the live show at Loew's
With the Voodoo Sex Queens from Outer Space.

Further out, beyond the Superdome, he would hear
The Natchez Queen puffing up the river
Like an athlete out of shape,

Or hitch a ride on the fabled train
Chugging through the heavy evening air,
Rich dark laughter
Shining like gold in an alley.
He would smell the sea and Lake Pontchartrain
Perfume and sweat, chicory, trash and magnolias,
Catalogue the whorls on an oyster shell.

Later he might loaf along the levees
Stroke their voluptuous shoulders
Take his ease under oaks and sleepy cypresses,
Spanish moss trailing from their limbs
Like tattered shawls.
He would pass
Through both the shotgun shacks
And antebellum dowagers of the Garden District
Becoming part of them,
Of everything.

Then, under a starry night
He would watch the endless pageant
Of streaming lights
To find his way to Duncan Plaza
Where Avery Alexander points the way,
Leaning into civil rights
And remembering the auction block,
Where John McDonough wants to do
"Good, much good, great good"
For his fellow man.

At last Walt would stretch out
By the homeless man
Asleep at the feet of George Washington
And dream,
Curled into the heart
Of New Orleans,
Grimy jewel of the South
Glowing
In the foil
Of Big Muddy.

on charles whitman

August 1st was hazy.
Students ambled to their classes
In unwilling herds, books
Balanced on their hips.

Three blocks away
In our decrepit rooms
I struggled with a birthday cake,
Butter icing melting in the heat.

Inside the Tower
Carrels bulged with sluggish grads.
Traffic inched in lazy ribbons
Down the Drag.

No one saw
The ex-Marine
Who took the elevator
Far as it would go.

Summer oozed through walls
Crept up furniture.
I put the cake
Inside the fridge.

He reached the observation deck,
Unpacked deodorant and rifles
Ate some lunch.
No one saw

At first
The lazy puffs of smoke, or heard
Those dull reports
That sounded like a distant fireworks show.

No one made connection
Even when the passersby
Began to melt
Along the sidewalks

Or in front of cars
And smoke kept rising
From the Tower
In languid spirals

Almost festive, like the fumes
From blown-out candles
On a youngster's
Birthday cake.

They got it, finally.
Phones went off
In high electric screams
And sirens scattered noon.

Police cars raced
Along the streets
In frenzied lines
Like worker ants defending hills

Smashed by a giant mower.
I got a call
From someone penned
Inside the Co-op.

He told me
To take cover,
Told me
What I knew.

By nightfall
Heat had drained the campus
As the moon rose indolent
Above the blistered trees.

The cake
Had hardened in the fridge
Too stiff, too cold
To touch.

AT THE WORLD TRADE CENTER

Somewhere in the desert, dawn comes late
And angles of the world begin to shift
In acrid billows of free-floating hate.

Twin fireballs bloom like giant poppies, fate
Of millions melted down, consumed. Hands drift
Somewhere. In the desert dawn comes late

As reams of paper spin through light, gyrate.
Small dervishes in white, they drop and lift
In acrid billows of free-floating hate

While grimed firefighters plod through ruin, their gait
Slowed by the footsore dogs that whimper, sniff
Somewhere in the desert. Dawn comes late

Through crumpled girders, sirens, shouts, a spate
Of cell phones ringing in the labyrinth
On acrid billows of free-floating hate.

Now at the fuming crypt new mourners wait,
Light candles, listen for a breath, a gift.
Somewhere in the desert, dawn comes late
In acrid billows of free-floating hate.

New Fridge

My grandparents bought it during Viet Nam
When no one talked of anything but Tet.
They saved ten years to have this luxury
Ensconced it in our kitchen
Like an oracle. It brought forth
Myriad meals in a sweaty room,
Cooled our powdered milk and old roast beef
Thousands of miles

From those steamier jungles
Deadly green, drone of helicopters
Napalm blooming over palm trees.
We ate our meager suppers
Just before the nightly news
Roared through our living room,
Watched mud-stained infantry
Plod over armchairs, dodging mines and tables

Fording rivers on our carpet.
Finally we heard the casualty reports.
Later we would stuff left-overs
Back into the cold, wedge wrinkled grapes
Into their chilled compartments,
The next night burrowing
Through shelves like tunnel rats
Searching something fit to eat.

After the war and a twenty-year tour
The oracle came to me, suffered
The slings and arrows of a weary grunt
Churning valiantly with doors left open,
Ice trays running over
Magnets on the front
Bearing doctors' cards
And past-due bills.

Today we have a new one
And it runs like a sleek cat,
Its motor a complacent purr
But now the talk is all Iraq
And Lebanon, deserts, roadside bombs,
And I pack fish sticks in the freezer
Like soldiers
In Humvees.

Target Practice

Mother packed a Colt
Because she feared them,
Feared those midnight pilgrims
Stumbling through the tumbleweeds,
Sweat dried on their backs
Like a second skin
A few tortillas in a sack.

And so she lined us up
Each Saturday,
Tecate Mountain behind us
A fence line
Thirty feet in front,
Juice cans balanced
On each post.

No lunch until we shot them down
One by one,
Bird's Eye logos
Centered in our sights
Heavy steel wobbly
In our hands
The trigger hard to squeeze

But we brought them down
One by one
Shot after shot
Bullets ricocheting off the barn
Casings in the hay
We brought them down
Until one day

We saw those others, thin as twigs
Weightless as leaves
Weaving over the cattle guard
Like drunks dizzy in the morning air.
I felt the gun
Fall
To my side.

Piano

Mother bought it secondhand,
A grimy spinet
Shoved behind a Steinway.

We installed it in the living room
And she would play for hours,
A can of beer warming on the cheek block

Mazurkas and impromptus spinning
In a dusty cloud, eight-to-the-bar
Thumping in the works.

Chopin, Bach, and Liszt
Sat on our vinyl chairs
Hurling scores at her

And marginal corrections,
Beethoven helping her
Play "Für Elise."

Then I took over
Struggled through the Bach inventions
Sometimes a polonaise.

Soon children and grandchildren
Pounded it, chipped the keys,
Kicked the soundboard.

One child stuffed a toy dog
Into the action. Finally
The cover wouldn't close. I called

The tuner. He brushed off
Fifty years,
Cleaned the hammers. Suddenly

Bars of "Für Elise"
Jumped from the keyboard,
Strains of Mozart

Floating upward from the pedals
And I almost saw
My mother
Thumbing scores and turning pages
Hunting for the perfect piece,
A warm beer in her hand.

TaTTOO

for Adam

My face is drilled into my son
Life size
In shades of ochre, flame, and blue.
I think of needles, dyes
The artist saying things like "Raise your arm,"
"Keep still" or "Good work isn't cheap.
Cheap work isn't good"
While he extracts
From muscle
Curls and bright coronas
Set around my face

But not my face,
Not my features now
Their contours drooping into time.
Instead the artist works in memory
A crinkled photograph
Taken thirty years ago
When I was first engaged.
I smile into the future
Knowing nothing that would come
Backlight shooting rays
Into my new-permed hair.

The face that slowly surfaces
Beneath the needle
Is not mine
But his
Those untried bones, taut lines.
The artist adds another swirl
And we are canonized
My son and I
Unlikely sainthood
Radiant
Along his spine.

I ponder this apotheosis.
My face then
Is his face now, his is mine
Replicated in the visage
I once had.
I see my days
Now moving in reverse.
We lose time recover it
Lose it again in double progress
Sooner, later, sweeping both of us
Beyond the picture.

Ballade of the Nutcracker Matinee

My grandchild wriggles in her seat and whines
For candy bars until the trumpets bore
Into the theater. A spotlight shines
And curtains rise as dancers take the floor
To spin into the famous story, pore
Over their gifts, and dream. No longer tired,
She quickly learns good timing, narrow door,
That line between the real and the aspired.

This afternoon it's perfect. Clara finds
Her Prince. They oust the Mouse King and restore
The Sugar Plums. She pirouettes twelve times,
Twirls ecstatically. And when they soar
Into the *pas de deux*, that magic core
Of Clara's night, the cast looks on, beguiled
As he catches her midair, ends the war,
That line between the real and the aspired.

Years hence, when they have aged and each joint grinds,
Legs thickened like old gravy, life a chore
The Prince's hands reduced to nervous vines,
When my grandchild ponders the murky lore
Of Tchaikovsky's depression, ghosts that roar
On every page of script, his genius mired
In doubt and darkness, she'll love all the more
That line between the real and the aspired

Recalling a December day that tore
Through time, a day when we were weightless, wired
To float onstage, our toes poised to explore
That line between the real and the aspired.

ELECTION DAY, 2008

Who would have believed
In Lincoln's bloody land,
Places where nooses
Hung from giant oaks
Like alien Spanish moss
That such a thing could be?

Who would have guessed
Where sharecroppers in cotton fields
Lived and died on molasses and mush
While others froze in miles of crumbling brick,
Broken glass and free-range rats
That such a time could come?

Who would have thought
So many could travel
Down paths worn smooth by night-riders
Past burning crosses, water fountains
And polling places out of reach
To find a place in the front of the bus?

Yet on this day
A jubilee began: hymns rolled down like rivers
From the fire hoses, dreams rose
From the muzzles of rifles, flowers sprouted
Out of manacles
And all the police dogs
Bayed hallelujah
In a chorus no one will forget.

HOW TO STOP war

Put Yo Yo Ma in every doorway,
Pavarotti at each checkpoint
Perlman on the road to Kosovo
Or in Rwanda's thick green hills.

Let the hands of Artur Rubinstein
Float slowly over Belfast
Have Marsalis
Shoot cadenzas into Gaza.

When they fill the bores
Of AK 47s
With scores of Brandenburg concertos,
When we arm the Stealths with Mozart

No one will hear the voices
Calling them to blood. Remastered,
They will find their families
Building ballads in the streets,

See them tuning old guitars
Inside their tents,
Chords shimmering
In Kabul's radiant dust

Rising
Past
The minefields
Into melodies.

Family Gathering

In my dream
I'm looking at a crinkled photo
Taken Easter Sunday
In an unknown year.
Faces come into sharp focus
Vanish, reappear
In endless rounds.
Fade in
Fade out.

Mother hasn't had her stroke
Or is that Grandmother
With the tired blue eyes, her veined arms
Wrapped around a great-grandchild
Who's just learned how to walk?
Is that my daughter's baby? Mine?
My sister is still pregnant
With a second girl,
Or is that child a boy? Her first or third?

Now I'm in the picture.
Caught between these overlapping lives
I show off
A yellow linen suit,
Stand with my son
And his new girlfriend.
Lilies drift in random progress
Past the frame.
Fade in, fade out.

Brothers, husbands join us,
Stare responsibly into the lens
But now it's 1943.
My father, a Marine, cradles me
While I squall at the top of my new lungs
And his mother leaves off
Building fighter planes

To smile at us admiringly.
Or is that man my son?

I want to walk out of this portrait
And its decades floating by
In blurry pageants
But the others pull me back
Into their shimmering tableaux
Of love
And loss
Played through uncertain light.
Fade in, fade out.

V

New Poems

BreakinG THe DrouGHT

We wait for rain
The way a sailor
On a long and dismal cruise
Might yearn
For the sight of land
Or the touch of his lover.

The sun, a daily juggernaut,
Grinds streets and skies to grit,
Turns earth to stone.
Grass dries to tawny skeletons
And trees drop branches
Like cast-off clothes.

Finally, when every leaf is charred
And no green can be seen for miles,
Rain comes. Bullfrogs morph
Into downsized elephants, trumpeting
In every puddle. Sage and bougainvillea
Bloom like hallucinations in red and indigo.

I stand in my yard, a temporary statue,
While the storm rolls down me, wave on wave
In a long embrace
And I feel wet grass beneath my feet,
An old friend
Come home at last.

Fracking in South Texas

When I drive to the Valley,
It's mile on mile
Of heat and mesquite,
A steady beat
Of sun and prickly pear,
Steam rising off the blacktop
In an endless breath
Until I leave the interstate
And head south for Three Rivers.
There the roadbed
Starts to crack and sink
Beneath the weight
Of Macks and giant rigs,
Air travel and AC.

Sandwiched at the stoplight
Between two eighteen-wheelers,
Dozens more ahead, behind
I look at their freight—
Those pipes three feet across, those drums
Of unnamed liquid,
Those girders, jacks and pumps—

And I start to think
About their destinations,
The spaces they will fill.
Whose water will catch fire?
Which rancher's back
Or spleen or pancreas
Will sprout strange growths,
Whose fields
Will heave and shake
With seismic fever,
Whose Herefords
Will fall sick,
Their bodies bloating in the sun
Before I reach George West?

Lincoln in an Upscale Mall

I imagine him in this place
That bears his name, taking a break
From rail-splitting
To sip a latte at Starbucks
Or easing his gangly frame
Into an armchair
At Barnes & Noble
To pore over volumes of the law,
Fine-tune his Gettysburg Address.

Then the Great Emancipator
Might cross the parking lot
In long, lanky strides
To buy a pair of Birkenstocks
For his five-mile walk
To return a book, stopping on the way
At Whole Foods to get
Some free-range chicken
And gluten-free cookies for his mother.

Next it's on to Chico's
To choose a designer scarf
For Mary Todd,
Maybe a little something
At Victoria's Secret,
A brief stop at Toy Express
To pick up hoverboards
And LEGOS
For his sons

Before he returns to his barge
And poles it down the Missouri,
Churning up a wash of mud and guns
Iron manacles
And blood-stained cotton bolls
Floating toward the banks,

Teeming hospitals and fragments
Of tents, past Springfield and New Salem,
Decades roiling in his wake.

Back at the mall
Customers crowd P.F. Chang's,
Chattering about the Kardashians
Over their chopsticks
While the Sixteenth President
Trims his scraggly beard, lines seaming
His raw-boned face like tributaries
Of a great river, finally
Puts on a boiled dress shirt
For an evening at the theater.

During a Polar Vortex

Shivering in a parka
And fleece-lined gloves,
I've walked down my driveway
Three nights now
To catch the show,

That luscious butter moon.
A radiant queen
Left alone after her cosmic party,
I've watched her float
Slowly

Down the western sky,
Watched her coat
First the heavens, then
My neighbor's rooftop,
His ice-tipped oaks

In their bare-branch filigree,
Finally his frozen grass
With light,
Largesse of creamy light
Enfolding everything,

Serendipity of warmth
In so much cold.

Navigating Mexico

We drive through village
After thirsty village,
Down dusty streets
With walls on either side,
Miles of walls, adobe or cinderblock
Blank as a closed eye.

Some have glass or razor wire
On top. A few are staked
With palisades, iron spikes
Pointing up, hours of walls
Broken now and then
By gates with heavy hinges.

In Chiapas, one boy
Points an imaginary gun at us,
And fires.
A woman in Oaxaca looks up
From her murky wash
To scowl. One man throws a rock.

Walled off
Almost from each other,
We reach our hotel at dusk.
One gate opens
And the world
Dazzles into green.

Ferns hang in swaying baskets,
Fronds drooping like skirts
Of resting dancers.
Bougainvillea and lemon trees
Spiral up toward night,
Their leaves fat like jovial tycoons

And in the center
Of the fragrant dark

A fountain purls and shimmers,
Iridescent droplets everywhere
Cooling our sunburned faces
And boiling blood
Like a mother's calm embrace.

venice

for Sara, David, and Grahame

She'll take us in the end, just as she has
Her other conquests for twelve centuries
But we won't mind. All sequins, fierce gold curls,
She'll watch us while we plod across a bridge
And lose our way in dark streets three feet wide,
No windows, pave stones hard beneath our feet.
Her lions at her side, she'll thread a course
Around the stalls and warring gondolas
To meet her friend Lord Byron, taking off
Her fine black leather boots to swim with him
Across the wide lagoon, through brackish streams
And byways, always leading by a stroke,
A trail of light and glitter in her wake.

She'll be there every morning when we drink
Our cappuccino, sugar and thick cream
A warm glaze on our lips. She'll know when we
Decide to buy those shoddy T-shirts made
In China at a kiosk near St. Mark's,
Take selfies at the Bridge of Sighs, or catch
A vaporetto headed the wrong way.
She'll see us stumble through cathedrals, gape
At gold leaf and mosaics, miracles
And deaths. She'll listen when the doge metes out
His words of justice for Othello, note
When Shylock fails to get his pound of flesh.

We never view her fully. She will keep
Her head in profile, often veiled, a mask
From Carnevale in her hand. At night
She'll keep a vigil by the sea, serene,
Renew deep Adriatic vows each year,
Her gold ring thrown into its murky waves.
And only when we board the jet for home,
Approach our cruising altitude, will she
Reveal herself in full, the Grand Canal
Caressing her bright body, spellbound, rapt,
A lover who can't bear to say goodbye.

An Evening with Willie Nelson

for Adam

In the arena at 80,
He leaves his glossy pickup and climbs
Illuminated stairs to reach
The revolving stage, jumbotrons above him,
And pour out his odyssey
For cheering crowds. Songs stream
From everywhere, the circle unbroken.
He's on the road again, with blue eyes
Crying in the rain and Georgia
On his mind. So are whisky river
And the City of New Orleans.

So much still is left:
His grizzled beard
And long gray braids
Those gnarled hands and lean arms,
The trademark red bandanna.
I think about Ulysses
In his last years
Sailing west, past assorted storms
And rival deities, Poseidon and Calypso,
Telemachus and even Penelope
Knowing he would not return.

Soon we'll all fly away
But I have a fluorescent longhorn
Stamped on my hand
To show me where I am
And where I've been
As I too follow the sun
And sail west.

ACKNOWLEDGMENTS

The author acknowledges with gratitude the following periodicals and anthologies in which some of these poems first appeared:

Acequia 1992 and 1994, *Atlanta Review, Blue Unicorn, Borderlands, CCTE Studies* 2000 and 2003, *The Chaffin Journal, Coal City Review, Concho River Review, Context South, descant, diverse-city* 2000, *English Journal, The Formalist, Goodbye, Mexico: Poems of Remembrance, Green Hills Literary Lantern, Illya's Honey, Inlet, Iron Horse Literary Review, Journal of Texas Women Writers, Langdon Review* 2005 and 2018, *The Larger Geometry: Poems for Peace, New Texas* 1995, 2001, and 2012, *The Paisano, RE Arts & Letters, Red River Review, Revista/Review Interamericana, riverSedge* 1991 and 1995, *San Antonio Express-News, San José Studies, SCOL: A Journal of the Texas College English Association, Southwestern American Literature* 1993 and 1995, *Texas Observer, Texas Poetry Calendar* 2007, 2008, and 2019, *Trinity Review, Valparaiso Poetry Review, Voices de la Luna, The Windhover,* and *Windows.*

ABOUT THE AUTHOR

Carol Coffee Reposa's work reflects the wide diversity of her life experience as a wife, mother, grandmother, teacher, traveler, musician, gardener, swimmer, and lifelong lover of the arts. Although born in Southern California, she comes from an unabashedly Texan family, and her work draws heavily on the history, culture, and climate of the Lone Star State. Author of four books of poetry and a four-time Pushcart Prize nominee, Reposa was a finalist in the *Malahat Review*'s long poem contest, winner of the Guadalupe Cultural Art Center's poetry contest (1992), and winner of the San Antonio Public Library's Arts & Letters Award (2015). She has also received three Fulbright-Hays Fellowships for study in Russia, Peru, Ecuador, and Mexico. The 2008 Texas Poet Laureate Larry Thomas describes her as a "national poet of seriousness and distinction." A member of the Texas Institute of Letters and the 2018 Texas Poet Laureate, Carol Coffee Reposa makes her home in San Antonio.